# DISAPPEARING
# Acts

## A SEARCH-AND-find
## BOOK OF Endangered ANIMALS

### Isabella
### BUNNELL

# ENDANGERED MOUNTAINS

MOUNTAIN GORILLA

SNOW LEOPARD

MOUNTAIN PYGMY POSSUM

GIANT PANDA

AMUR LEOPARD

# ENDANGERED RAINFOREST

GOLDEN LION TAMARIN
MONKEY

HYACINTH
MACAW

JAGUAR

GORILLA

SUMAN
ORANGUTAN

# ENDANGERED REEF

ELKHORN **CORAL**

SOCIAL **WRASSE**

GREEN-SEA **TURTLE**

BARBOUR'S **SEAHORSE**

# DUGONG

# ENDANGERED DESERT

SANDHILL
DUNNART

RIVERINE
RABBIT

DESERT
TORTOISE

BILBY

ADDAX

# ENDANGERED CAVES

FREE TAILED FIJAN BAT

WHITE-HEADED LANGUR

KANTHAN CAVE TRAPDOOR SPIDER

CAVE SQUEAKER

WOOLLY FLYING SQUIRREL

# ENDANGERED FRESHWATER

CAMPBELL'S
ALLIGATOR
LIZARD

LAYSAN
DUCK

GIANT
SALMON
CARP

ASIAN
SMALL CLAWED
OTTER

AMERICAN EEL

# ENDANGERED SKIES

**YELLOW EARED PARROT**

**GUNDLACH'S HAWK**

**MOUSTACHED KINGFISHER**

**YELLOW SHOULDERED BLACKBIRD**

**TALAUD FRUIT BAT**

# ENDANGERED GRASSLANDS

ONE HORNED
**RHINO**

BENGAL
**TIGER**

**BLACK
RHINO**

BLACK FOOTED
**FERRET**

**AFRICAN
ELEPHANT**

# ENDANGERED UNDERGROUND

NUMBAT

PURPLE PIG NOSED FROG

GIANT ARMADILLO

CHINESE PANGOLIN

GIANT GIPPSLAND WORM

# ENDANGERED OCEAN

HUMPHEAD
**WRASSE**

GIANT
DEVIL
RAY

SOUTHERN
BLUEFIN
**TUNA**

LEATHERBACK
**TURTLE**

SCALLOPED
HAMMERHEAD
**SHARK**

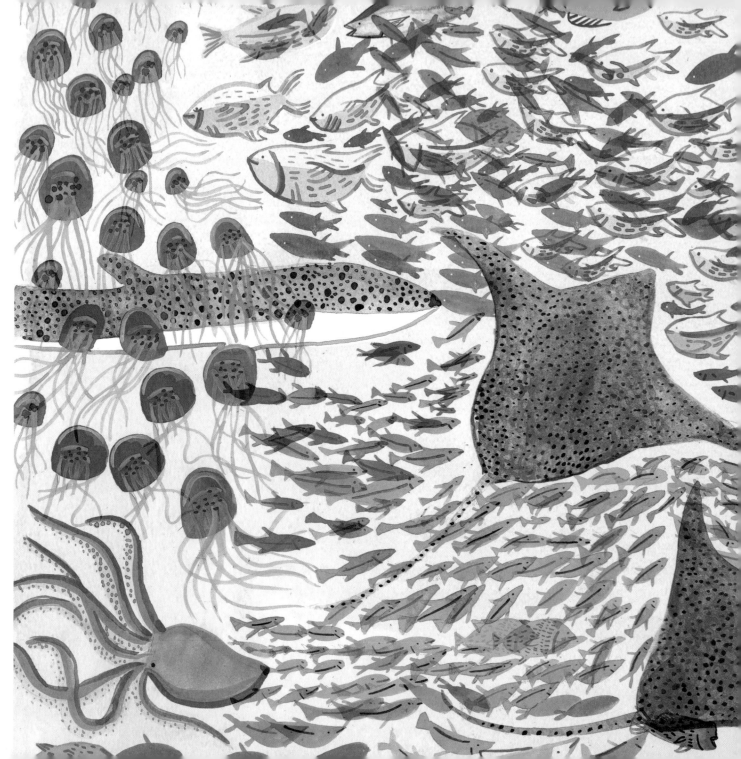

# ENDANGERED MOUNTAINS

## MOUNTAIN GORILLA

**FOUND IN**
Mountainous areas in Central Africa and Uganda

**NUMBERS LEFT**
Around 900

**ABOUT**
The mountain gorilla has longer fur than other gorillas, to suit the cold. They live in groups of one male and lots of females. When young male gorillas reach the age of 11, they leave the group to travel with an all-male pack until they are old enough to attract a group of females.

**WHY THEY ARE ENDANGERED**
Burning and logging of the mountain forests means there is less habitat for the mountain gorillas.

## SNOW LEOPARD

**FOUND IN**
The mountains of South East Asia

**NUMBERS LEFT**
Around 5,000

**ABOUT**
Despite its name, the snow leopard is more closely related to the tiger than the leopard. It has a short body with stocky limbs and small ears, to reduce heat loss. Its long, fat tail helps it balance on the rocky mountain slopes. At night, the snow leopard wraps its tail around its face to keep warm.

**WHY THEY ARE ENDANGERED**
Global warming and the farming of the lower mountain slopes means there is less prey for the snow leopards to eat.

## MOUNTAIN PYGMY POSSUM

**FOUND IN**
Southern Australia

**NUMBERS LEFT**
1,800

**ABOUT**
A tiny marsupial with big eyes and a small snout. It has a long tail, which is prehensile, meaning it can grab things. It is nocturnal and mostly feeds on a diet of Bogong moths, nuts and seeds.

**WHY THEY ARE ENDANGERED**
The development of ski resorts in its mountain habitat is a big threat. Predators such as the red fox and wild cat are becoming more common. Also Bogong moths, which make up most of its diet, are becoming rarer.

## GIANT PANDA

**FOUND IN**
The mountains of Central China

**NUMBERS LEFT**
Around 1,500

**ABOUT**
This gentle bear has the body of a carnivore, but is almost completely vegetarian, eating around 11kg of bamboo every day. Because of its limited diet, the panda is quite a slow, lazy creature. It is not very sociable, and doesn't venture far from its small territory.

**WHY THEY ARE ENDANGERED**
Loss of habitat was a big problem, but scientists now believe panda populations are slowly growing.

## AMUR LEOPARD

**FOUND IN**
The mountains of Southeast Russia/ Northeast China

**NUMBERS LEFT**
Around 60

**ABOUT**
The amur leopard is the most endangered big cat in the world. It has a thick, creamy coat of fur, which protects it against the bitter Siberian winters. It has a relatively small body and a distinctive pattern of widely spaced spots.

**WHY THEY ARE ENDANGERED**
Destruction of habitat and poaching are the two main threats. Because there are so few amur leopards left, breeding is tricky.

# ENDANGERED RAINFOREST

## JAGUAR

**FOUND IN**
Central and South America

**NUMBERS LEFT**
Around 15,000

**ABOUT**
The jaguar looks like a big, stocky leopard. It is a stalk-and-ambush predator, which means that rather than chasing its prey, it hides and pounces. It is a strong swimmer and climber and has a very powerful bite.

**WHY THEY ARE ENDANGERED**
The jaguar needs large areas of rainforest and riverbank to survive. It was once found throughout Central and South America, but is now mostly limited to the Amazon Rainforest.

## GOLDEN LION TAMARIN

**FOUND IN**
Brazil's Atlantic coastal forests

**NUMBERS LEFT**
Around 3,200

**ABOUT**
This little monkey gets its name from the mane of bright red hair that frames its face. It has sharp, claw-like nails that help it cling onto branches as it scampers through the trees eating fruit and drinking nectar.

**WHY THEY ARE ENDANGERED**
Only around 3% of the Atlantic forests are still standing. The tamarins have been successfully introduced elsewhere and their population is gradually growing.

## HYACINTH MACAW

**FOUND IN**
Central and Eastern South America

**NUMBERS LEFT**
2,500 in the wild

**ABOUT**
The hyacinth macaw is the largest parrot in the world. It is completely blue except for a tiny bit of yellow skin around its eyes. It has a big strong beak, perfect for cracking coconuts and macadamia nuts. It is sometimes kept as a pet, due to its sweet, calm nature.

**WHY THEY ARE ENDANGERED**
The loss of habitat to farmland and logging has brought the numbers down. Hyacinth macaws fetch a high price as pets, so are a target for poachers.

## CROSS RIVER GORILLA

**FOUND IN**
Cameroon-Nigeria border

**NUMBERS LEFT**
Around 250

**ABOUT**
The cross river gorilla is a type of western lowland gorilla with light brown fur and a relatively small head. It lives on fruit and tree bark and makes nests on the ground and in trees. It is the only gorilla species in this region that is known to use tools.

**WHY THEY ARE ENDANGERED**
Habitat loss means that the population has halved in the past 20 years – one of the most radical declines of any ape population.

## SUMATRAN ORANGUTAN

**FOUND IN**
Indonesia

**NUMBERS LEFT**
Around 6,700

**ABOUT**
The orangutan is the most intelligent of the great apes, using sophisticated tools to get insects out of holes and open nuts. A mother organutan will look after her child for a full two years. Orangutans have stocky bodies with long, strong arms and short legs – perfect for swinging through trees. Some adult males have big cheek pads to mark them out as powerful.

**WHY THEY ARE ENDANGERED**
Habitat destruction and poaching are the two main threats.

# ENDANGERED REEF

## ELKHORN CORAL

**FOUND IN**
The Caribbean

—

**NUMBERS LEFT**
85% less than 30 years ago

—

**ABOUT**
Elkhorn coral is a big, brownish coral that grows in warm, shallow waters. It has big branches, reaching two metres wide that look like elk antlers. It offers an important habitat to many fish and shellfish species.

—

**WHY THEY ARE ENDANGERED**
Coral diseases, such as white pox, can spread quickly through elkhorn coral colonies. Coral eating snails and climate change have also caused damage to elkhorn reefs.

## SOCIAL WRASSE

**FOUND IN**
Belize Barrier Reef, Caribbean

—

**NUMBERS LEFT**
Unknown

—

**ABOUT**
This little fish is brightly coloured, with an orange body, white undercarriage and a blue tail fin. It lives in the shallow coral reef, feeding on small sea insects. It has big lips and separate jaw teeth that jut outwards.

—

**WHY THEY ARE ENDANGERED**
The unique mangrove-reef habitat in which the young wrasses develop is threatened. Their main predator, the lionfish, has become more common.

## GREEN-SEA TURTLE

**FOUND IN**
Warm areas of the Atlantic and Pacific

—

**NUMBERS LEFT**
Around 90,000 nesting female turtles

—

**ABOUT**
One of the biggest turtles in the world, the green sea turtle has a wide shell, a flat body and big flippers. Its name comes not from the colour of it shell, which is normally brownish, but from the layer of green fat under its shell.

—

**WHY THEY ARE ENDANGERED**
Turtle meat and eggs are considered a delicacy in some parts of the worlds. When nesting beaches get built up, there is nowhere for the turtles to lay their eggs.

## BARBOUR'S SEAHORSE

**FOUND IN**
Indonesia, Malaysia and the Phillipines

—

**NUMBERS LEFT**
Unknown

—

**ABOUT**
This seahorse lives in shallow seagrass beds. It has a long, narrow snout, a short tail and a high crown of spikes on its head. Although they are a type of fish, seahorses don't have scales, but rather thin skin stretched over bony plates. The male seahorse looks after the eggs in a pouch on his stomach.

—

**WHY THEY ARE ENDANGERED**
Seahorses are slow swimmers, making them an easy target for predators and poachers. Trawlers cause damage to their habitat.

## DUGONG

**FOUND IN**
Pacific and Indian Oceans

—

**NUMBERS LEFT**
2,250

—

**ABOUT**
The dugong, or sea cow, is the only vegetarian sea mammal in the world. It has a long snout with a wide, curved mouth, covered with sensitive bristles. It grazes on underwater grasses day and night. Its name comes from the Malay word *duyung*, meaning 'lady of the sea'. It is a close relative of the elephant.

—

**WHY THEY ARE ENDANGERED**
This slow creature makes easy prey, and was traditionally hunted for its meat and oil. They have low reproduction levels.

# ENDANGERED DESERT

## SANDHILL DUNNART

—
**FOUND IN**
The deserts of Southern Australia

—
**NUMBERS LEFT**
Around 100

—
**ABOUT**
These mouse-like marsupials have big ears and thick tails in which they store fat. They live in the desert dunes, taking shelter from the heat by building burrows under hummocks of Spinifex grass. They eat insects such as ants, beetles and termites.

—
**WHY THEY ARE ENDANGERED**
There is a decline in Spinifex grass, and so their habitat is threatened.

## RIVERINE RABBIT

—
**FOUND IN**
The Karoo Desert, South Africa

—
**NUMBERS LEFT**
Around 250

—
**ABOUT**
A rabbit with long ears and a long, grey body. It has black stripes on its face and white rings around its eyes. It is a nocturnal animal, sleeping during the day in shallow burrows hidden under bushes, and venturing out at night to eat flowers, grasses and leaves.

—
**WHY THEY ARE ENDANGERED**
Habitat loss and accidental trapping by hunters.

## DESERT TORTOISE

—
**FOUND IN**
United States and Northern Mexico

—
**NUMBERS LEFT**
Unknown

—
**ABOUT**
These tough creatures survive the dramatic desert temperatures by spending 98% of their time in burrows under the soil, coming out only early in the morning and at dusk to feed on shrubs and cacti. In the heat of the summer they survive on water stored in their bodies.

—
**WHY THEY ARE ENDANGERED**
Loss of habitat and an explosion in the population of ravens, who prey on tortoise eggs.

## BILBY

—
**FOUND IN**
Australia

—
**NUMBERS LEFT**
600

—
**ABOUT**
Around the size of a rabbit, the bilby has a long, pointy nose, grey fur, a black and white tail and huge ears that let out heat. These marsupials build deep, spiral-shaped burrows in which they sleep during the day. After dark, they forage for plants and insects with their long, skinny tongues.

—
**WHY THEY ARE ENDANGERED**
Habitat loss and new predators such as foxes and cats have wiped out a lot of the bilby population.

## ADDAX

—
**FOUND IN**
The Sahara Desert

—
**NUMBERS LEFT**
500

—
**ABOUT**
This antelope is well-adapted to the desert. It has white fur that reflects the sun and it can live without water for long periods of time. Addaxes roam around in small herds of up to 20 members, led by the oldest female. Their horns have a wavy, spiral shape.

—
**WHY THEY ARE ENDANGERED**
The addax is a slow moving creature and is an easy target for hunters and predators.

# ENDANGERED CAVES

## FREE TAILED FIJAN BAT

**FOUND IN**
Fiji and Vaanutu

**NUMBERS LEFT**
Unknown

**ABOUT**
This bat has long narrow wings and an interesting retractable tail that helps it steer while flying. It is one of the fastest flying bats.

**WHY THEY ARE ENDANGERED**
There are only three known roosting caves for these rare bats, one of which is in danger of collapsing, as it is underneath a busy road.

## KANTHAN CAVE TRAPDOOR SPIDER

**FOUND IN**
Gunung Kanthan Cave in Malaysia

**NUMBERS LEFT**
Unknown

**ABOUT**
The trapdoor spider doesn't live in a web. Instead, it lives in a burrow that is camouflaged with mud. At the entrance to the burrow, it builds a hard door with silk hinges on one side and silk 'trip wires' coming out of it. The spider waits in its burrow and when its prey triggers a trip wire, it leaps out of the trapdoor, catches it, and drags it inside the burrow.

**WHY THEY ARE ENDANGERED**
This spider is only known to exist in one cave in Malaysia, which is at risk of collapse because of quarrying.

## WHITE-HEADED LANGUR

**FOUND IN**
Cat Ba Island, Vietnam

**NUMBERS LEFT**
64

**ABOUT**
One of the rarest primates in the world, the white-headed langur lives in the caves of the steep limestone cliffs of Cat Ba Island. They are mostly black with white heads, cheeks and necks. They have a tail almost twice as long as their bodies to help them climb and balance.

**WHY THEY ARE ENDANGERED**
The langur is hunted for use in traditional medicine. Tourism on Cat Ba Island means that the remote cliffs will soon become easily accessed by poachers.

## CAVE SQUEAKER

**FOUND IN**
Zimbabwe

**NUMBERS LEFT**
Unknown

**ABOUT**
This tiny frog measures just 25mm. It is brown with black speckles, and bands on its legs. It is one of the few frog species that do not metamorphose from tadpoles. Instead, the frog hatches from its egg as a miniature adult. This means that the eggs do not have to be laid in water – just in a damp location.

**WHY THEY ARE ENDANGERED**
The frogs live in a very small area, which is threatened by mining.

## WOOLLY FLYING SQUIRREL

**FOUND IN**
Northern Pakistan

**NUMBERS LEFT**
Around 2,000

**ABOUT**
A very large flying squirrel that can reach 65cm long. It has thick, woolly fur, and, like other flying squirrels, it has a membrane between its front and back legs that acts as a parachute, allowing it to glide between trees. It lives in cliff caves in Pakistan's pine forests

**WHY THEY ARE ENDANGERED**
The pine forests are being cleared, resulting in habitat loss.

# ENDANGERED FRESHWATER

## CAMPBELL'S ALLIGATOR LIZARD

–
**FOUND IN**
Guatemala

–
**NUMBERS LEFT**
Around 500

–
**ABOUT**
This secretive, tree-dwelling lizard lives in the cloud forests of Guatemala. It has a wedge-shaped head and ridges along each of its sides, running from the corner of its mouth to its tail. It has brownish skin with large scales that can be shed in one piece like a snake. If caught, it has a sharp, painful bite.

–
**WHY THEY ARE ENDANGERED**
Loss of habitat and poaching for the pet trade.

## LAYSAN DUCK

–
**FOUND IN**
Laysan Island, Hawaii

–
**NUMBERS LEFT**
Around 500

–
**ABOUT**
This very small, dark duck has a white ring around its eyes and a layer of fat around its neck. It is a good runner, and will dash along mudflats, snapping at the rising cloud of flies with its stubby green beak.

–
**WHY THEY ARE ENDANGERED**
These ducks evolved with no real predators, and when faced with danger they tend to freeze, making them easy prey. Disease and habitat loss have also taken their toll.

## GIANT SALMON CARP

–
**FOUND IN**
The Mekong River in Laos and Cambodia

–
**NUMBERS LEFT**
Unknown

–
**ABOUT**
This big freshwater fish can reach 1.3m long and up to 30kg. It lives in the deep rapids of the Mekong River, swimming upstream to spawn.

–
**WHY THEY ARE ENDANGERED**
Once very common, overfishing and the construction of dams have brought the numbers of giant salmon carp down by 90% in the last 20 years.

## ASIAN SMALL CLAWED OTTER

–
**FOUND IN**
The wetlands of India and South East Asia

–
**NUMBERS LEFT**
Around 5,000

–
**ABOUT**
This little, slender otter has short claws, which means it can catch crabs and shellfish with its agile paws instead of with its mouth. Relative to other otters, it has a long tail and a short neck and is a very fast swimmer.

–
**WHY THEY ARE ENDANGERED**
These otters mostly live in mangrove swamps, which are threatened by habitat destruction and pollution.

## AMERICAN EEL

–
**FOUND IN**
East coast of the USA

–
**NUMBERS LEFT**
Unknown

–
**ABOUT**
A snake-like fish with scales so small that it seems completely smooth. It lives in the freshwater systems of the Hudson and St Lawrence rivers, leaving the rivers and bays to spawn in the Saragasso Sea. It hides in mud close to the shore during the day, emerging at night to hunt shellfish and small water insects.

–
**WHY THEY ARE ENDANGERED**
Hydroelectric dams have blocked the eels' spawning migrations. Fishing and disease have also had an impact.

# ENDANGERED SKIES

## YELLOW EARED PARROT

**FOUND IN**
Columbia and Ecuador

**NUMBERS LEFT**
Around 1,100

**ABOUT**
This parrot looks a bit like a like a macaw, with similar yellow ear-patches and underparts. It is quite big with a bright green body and a long tail. It nests in the hollow trunks of wax palms, and eats bark, buds and fruit. It mates for life.

**WHY THEY ARE ENDANGERED**
The harvesting of wax palms has led to habitat loss.

## GUNDLACH'S HAWK

**FOUND IN**
Cuba

**NUMBERS LEFT**
Around 400

**ABOUT**
A small bird of prey with blue-grey wings, a pale grey body and big feet. Its stocky body is built for speed, and it is faster than most other hawks. The Gundlach's hawk only eats other birds, including Cuban parrots, doves, parakeets and quail.

**WHY THEY ARE ENDANGERED**
Logging and deforestation have led to loss of habitat.

## MOUSTACHED KINGFISHER

**FOUND IN**
Papua New Guinea

**NUMBERS LEFT**
Around 700

**ABOUT**
A beautiful kingfisher with a red bill, an orange underbelly and purple facial markings and wings. Its short tail, sharp eyesight and rounded wingtips make it a fast hunter, adept at swiping insects from the air. At dawn and dusk it makes a distinctive 'ko-ko-ko' laughing sound.

**WHY THEY ARE ENDANGERED**
Habitat loss.

## YELLOW SHOULDERED BLACKBIRD

**FOUND IN**
Puerto Rico

**NUMBERS LEFT**
Around 900

**ABOUT**
A glossy black bird with bright yellow patches on its shoulders. It builds its nests in mangrove trees or in cliffs, and gathers in flocks at communal feeding sites to feast on insects.

**WHY THEY ARE ENDANGERED**
These birds were once very common across Puerto Rico but since the 1900s, sugar cane plantations have led to loss of habitat. They are also vulnerable to parasites and disease.

## TALAUD FRUIT BAT

**FOUND IN**
The tropical swamps of Salebabu and Karekaleng, Indonesia

**NUMBERS LEFT**
Unknown

**ABOUT**
Also known as the talaud flying fox, this is a very big bat that feeds on nectar and fruit. Unlike bats that eat insects, these bats have very good eyesight and smell, and don't rely on echolocation to find their way around.

**WHY THEY ARE ENDANGERED**
Habitat loss.

# ENDANGERED
# GRASSLANDS

## ONE HORNED RHINO

–
**FOUND IN**
India and Nepal

–
**NUMBERS LEFT**
2,500

–
**ABOUT**
Also known as the Indian Rhino, this animal has thick grey skin and a single black horn. These rhinos are good swimmers and spend most of the day wallowing in ponds. Water gets trapped in their big skin folds and cools them down as they roam the grasslands.

–
**WHY THEY ARE ENDANGERED**
Poaching used to be a problem, but that is mostly no longer the case. Habitat loss is this rhino's biggest threat.

## BENGAL TIGER

–
**FOUND IN**
India, Bangladesh, Bhutan, Nepal

–
**NUMBERS LEFT**
2,500 in the wild

–
**ABOUT**
The largest of the cat species, the Bengal tiger has a distinctive orange coat with black camouflage stripes and a white belly. It is a powerful nocturnal hunter, preying on buffalo, deer, wild pigs and other large mammals. Tigers do not attack humans unless other food is scarce.  A hungry tiger can eat 25kg of meat in one night.

–
**WHY THEY ARE ENDANGERED**
Habitat loss and poaching are major threats to tigers.

## BLACK RHINO

–
**FOUND IN**
Angola, Kenya, Mozambique, South Africa, Tanzania, Zimbabwe

–
**NUMBERS LEFT**
Around 4,800

–
**ABOUT**
Both black rhinos and white rhinos are actually grey. The difference between them is not colour but lip shape; the black rhino has a pointed lip, suited to plucking leaves and fruit, while the white rhino has a flat lip for grazing grasses. Black rhinos have two horns. The front horn can grow up to 1.5m long!

–
**WHY THEY ARE ENDANGERED**
Rhino horns are very valuable and are poached for use in Chinese medicine.

## BLACK FOOTED FERRET

–
**FOUND IN**
South Dakota, Arizona and Wyoming

–
**NUMBERS LEFT**
295

–
**ABOUT**
This weasel-like animal has black feet and a black 'eye mask'. It has short legs and a long body, perfect for crawling into the narrow burrow complexes of its prey, the prairie dog. It sleeps in abandoned prairie dog burrows during the day and attacks at night, when the prairie dogs are sleeping.

–
**WHY THEY ARE ENDANGERED**
Prairie dogs are pests for farmers, and as their populations have declined, so have the black footed ferrets.

## AFRICAN ELEPHANT

–
**FOUND IN**
Sub-Saharan Africa

–
**NUMBERS LEFT**
Around 500,000

–
**ABOUT**
The largest land animals on Earth, African elephants weigh up to six tons. They have big ears that radiate heat, keeping them cool. They have long trunks with two 'lips' at the end, used to grab things. They roam great distances in family units, foraging for all the roots, grasses, fruit and bark that they need to sustain their huge bodies.

–
**WHY THEY ARE ENDANGERED**
Poaching for ivory and meat, as well as habitat loss.

# ENDANGERED UNDERGROUND

## NUMBAT

-
**FOUND IN**
Western Australia

-
**NUMBERS LEFT**
Around 900

-
**ABOUT**
This termite-eating marsupial has red fur and a bushy tail. Most termite-eaters have powerful legs and heavy claws that can break into concrete-like termite mounds. This little animal doesn't have those qualities, so has to use its sharp sense of smell to find out where the termites feed, capturing them with its long, sticky tongue.

-
**WHY THEY ARE ENDANGERED**
New predators, like the European red fox, feed on numbats. Bush fires cause loss of habitat.

## CHINESE PANGOLIN

-
**FOUND IN**
Nepal, Bhutan, India and China

-
**NUMBERS LEFT**
Unknown

-
**ABOUT**
Covered in hard scales, pangolins look a bit like reptiles but are mammals. Chinese pangolins are shy creatures, who live in underground burrows, emerging at night to hunt for termites. When they are startled, pangolins roll themselves into a ball for protection.

-
**WHY THEY ARE ENDANGERED**
Pangolin meat is considered a delicacy, and their scales are used in Chinese medicine, so they are vulnerable to poaching.

## PURPLE PIG NOSED FROG

-
**FOUND IN**
India

-
**NUMBERS LEFT**
Around 135

-
**ABOUT**
One of the planet's weirder looking animals, the purple pig-nosed frog has a tiny head with goggly eyes and a pig-like snout, perched on a bloated body. It has short, sturdy limbs that help it burrow into the soil. It lives and feeds underground, surviving on a diet of termites. It only surfaces during the monsoon for mating.

-
**WHY THEY ARE ENDANGERED**
Loss of forest habitat as agricultural land takes over.

## GIANT ARMADILLO

-
**FOUND IN**
Across South America

-
**NUMBERS LEFT**
Unknown

-
**ABOUT**
The armadillo is covered in strong, armoured plates. It has stocky limbs and huge claws, perfect for digging the long burrows in which it sleeps for up to 18 hours a day. At night it emerges to forage for termites, plants and fruit. The armadillo can reach 1.5m long and has 100 teeth – the most of any mammal in the world!

-
**WHY THEY ARE ENDANGERED**
The armadillo is hunted for its meat (which is said to taste of pork). It is also threatened by habitat loss.

## GIANT GIPPSLAND WORM

-
**FOUND IN**
Victoria, Australia

-
**NUMBERS LEFT**
Unknown

-
**ABOUT**
These giant worms can reach 3m long. They live deep burrows alongside stream banks. Although they rarely surface, they can sometimes be heard making a gurgling noise as they slither through their burrows. Gippsland worms have long lifespans of around 10 years.

-
**WHY THEY ARE ENDANGERED**
Farming and pollution have led to the destruction of their habitat. Because it takes them so long to mature, breeding levels are low.